SAVE OUR EARTH!
Climate Action Explained

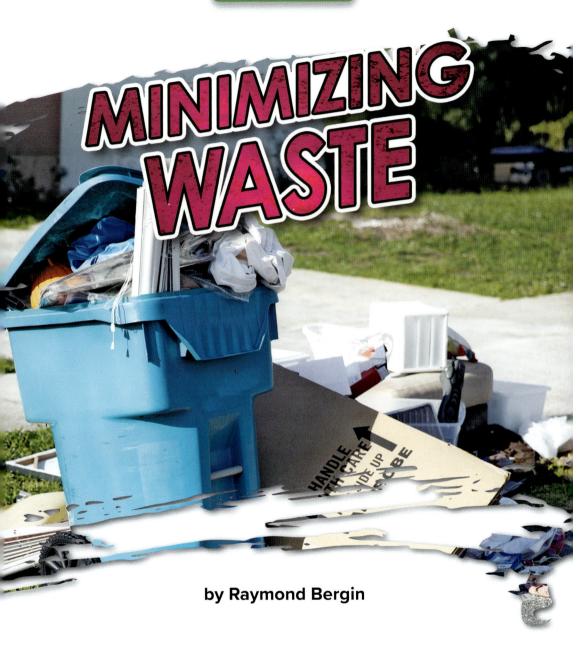

MINIMIZING WASTE

by Raymond Bergin

BEARPORT
PUBLISHING

Minneapolis, Minnesota

Credits
Cover and title page, © Tommy Doynjer/Shutterstock; 4–5, © Peter Gudella/Shutterstock; 7, © Bloomberg/Getty Images; 8, © Best-Backgrounds/Shutterstock; 8–9, © Tr Stok/Shutterstock; 10, © Algi Febri Sugita/Shutterstock; 10–11, © Ernest Rose/Shutterstock; 13, © Astrid Gast/Shutterstock; 14–15, © Flystock/Shutterstock; 17, © Tupungato/Shutterstock; 18–19, © Olga Yastremska/Adobe Stock; 20–21, © Circ/Geoff Wood Photography; 21BL, © Inditex/Zara Woman; 23, © Simon Maina/Getty Images; 24–25, © Justin Tallis/Getty Images; 26–27, © Eugenio Marongiu/Shutterstock; 28, © Ana Fernandez/SOPA Images/Associated Press; 29TL, © ArtMarie/iStock; 29UML, © zaiets roman/Adobe Stock; 29ML, © mixetto/iStock; 29BML, © SeventyFour/Shutterstock; 29BL, © Studio Romantic/Shutterstock

Bearport Publishing Company Product Development Team
Publisher: Jen Jenson; Director of Product Development: Spencer Brinker; Managing Editor: Allison Juda; Editor: Cole Nelson; Associate Editor: Tiana Tran; Production Editor: Naomi Reich; Designer: Kim Jones; Designer: Kayla Eggert; Designer: Steve Scheluchin; Production Specialist: Owen Hamlin

Statement on Usage of Generative Artificial Intelligence
Bearport Publishing remains committed to publishing high-quality nonfiction books. Therefore, we restrict the use of generative AI to ensure accuracy of all text and visual components pertaining to a book's subject. See BearportPublishing.com for details.

Library of Congress Cataloging-in-Publication Data is available at www.loc.gov or upon request from the publisher.

ISBN: 979-8-89577-052-8 (hardcover)
ISBN: 979-8-89577-169-3 (ebook)

Copyright © 2026 Bearport Publishing Company. All rights reserved. No part of this publication may be reproduced in whole or in part, stored in any retrieval system, or transmitted in any form or by any means, electronic, mechanical, photocopying, recording, or otherwise, without written permission from the publisher. Bearport Publishing is a division of FlutterBee Education Group.

For more information, write to Bearport Publishing, 3500 American Blvd W, Suite 150, Bloomington, MN 55431.

Contents

What a Waste!........................... 4
Made from Nature 6
Energy to Burn.......................... 8
Wasted Style........................... 10
Food for Thought 12
Plastic Is Not Fantastic................. 14
Rethink and Reuse: Circular Amsterdam ... 16
Free Stuff! Neighborhood Swap Days 18
Transforming Textiles: Circ.............. 20
From Table to Farm: Sanergy 22
Seaweed Solutions: Notpla 24
Waste Not, Want Not.................... 26

Minimize Waste! 28
Glossary............................... 30
Read More............................. 31
Learn More Online...................... 31
Index.................................. 32
About the Author 32

What a Waste!

Overflowing garbage cans line the streets. Many of the items peeking out from the bins look almost brand-new. The dumpsters behind the supermarket are filled with unopened packages of food and oddly shaped produce. Much of this food is still good, but it will never be eaten. Instead, all this waste will end up being burned in **incinerators** or piled high in **landfills**. What on Earth is going on here, and how can we fix it?

Globally, we currently throw away more than 2 billion tons (1.8 billion t) of goods annually. By 2050, this number is expected to top 3.8 billion tn. (3.5 billion t).

Made from Nature

We live in a world full of stuff. Everything we have, make, and grow on Earth takes natural resources. These are materials found in nature, including **fossil fuels**, metals, water, and plants.

Though there seems to be an endless supply of stuff, there aren't unlimited natural resources. Many of these resources are **nonrenewable**. Once they're used, they are gone. If we keep using natural resources at our current rate, we are at risk of running out.

> Our digital devices use many minerals and metals. Clothes are often made from plant and animal products. Oil is a fossil fuel that is turned into many of the plastic products we use every day.

Many metals and minerals are buried in the earth. We mine to get to these resources.

Energy to Burn

The process of turning natural resources into food and finished products requires a lot of energy. Most of the power for our farms and factories comes from burning oil, natural gas, and coal.

When these fossil fuels are burned, however, they release harmful gases into the **atmosphere**. Some of these, including **carbon dioxide**, are known as greenhouse gases. They trap heat around our planet, just as the walls of a greenhouse trap heat. Because of this, Earth is warming. The resulting climate change is causing unusual, extreme, and even deadly weather worldwide.

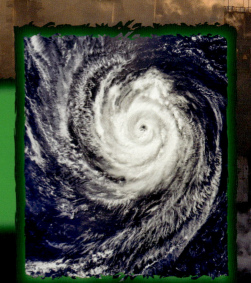

The effects of climate change on weather can be seen in increasingly powerful storms. Hurricanes, for example, grow larger and more quickly when ocean waters are warmer.

Wasted Style

Most products can be reused, repurposed, or recycled to prevent wasting the resources and energy that went into making them. Sadly, however, many things are quickly **disposed** of. This happens especially frequently in the fashion industry.

Worldwide, less than 1 percent of the material used to produce clothes is recycled into new clothing. More than 99 million tn. (90 million t) of **textiles** that could be recycled to make new garments are disposed of every year.

Many companies participate in fast fashion. They make and sell a lot of cheap, on-trend clothes that are not made to last. When the clothes are no longer in style, many of these garments are thrown away.

Food for Thought

Food waste is another global problem. About a fifth of all the food produced globally is thrown away or rots without being eaten. This waste is even more tragic in a world with millions of people starving.

In addition to the huge waste, the **decomposing** food is making the world hotter. As it breaks down, this waste releases the greenhouse gases carbon dioxide and **methane**. In fact, it is estimated that 8 to 10 percent of annual global greenhouse gas **emissions** come from food waste.

> Across Europe, 65 million tn. (59 million t) of food goes to waste every year. That amount could feed about 200 million people.

Plastic Is Not Fantastic

Plastic can be convenient, cheap, and versatile. However, it also is a huge part of our waste problem. Half of all plastic produced is tossed after only one use.

Single-use plastics are also a big litter problem. Water bottles, takeout containers, and straws clog beaches and waterways worldwide.

In addition to wasting resources, single-use plastic is harmful to nature. The fossil fuels and **toxic** chemicals used to make plastic pollute the air, water, and soil. Once thrown out, plastic decomposes slowly, **leaching** chemicals into the environment. Traces of poisonous plastic are now found in Earth's water, air, soil, and even in the bodies of people and other animals!

Many plastics are recyclable. However, less than 10 percent of the plastic ever made has been recycled. Instead, most of it ends up in landfills where it takes up to 1,000 years to break down.

Rethink and Reuse
Circular Amsterdam

The world is awash in waste. Fortunately, many people are thinking creatively about how to combat the problem.

With its Circular Amsterdam program, the capital of the Netherlands is the world's first city to embrace a circular economy. This means the community hopes to create a system using no new resources to make products. To do this, the government works with businesses and citizens to repair, repurpose, or recycle products that are breaking down. The government program also aims to reduce waste by eliminating plastic containers, **composting** food waste, and reusing building materials.

> After the program's first year, half of all Amsterdam residents had bought something at a second-hand store. About 70 percent had a product repaired instead of throwing it out.

Flea markets are popular shopping destinations in Amsterdam.

Free Stuff!
Neighborhood Swap Days

The city of Ann Arbor, Michigan, has also stepped up to combat waste. As part of its strategy to reduce greenhouse gas emissions and landfill load, the city hosts neighborhood swap days. Residents place unwanted items on their lawn for people to trade for or take away for free. Everything from clothes and books to furniture and appliances have their useful lives extended in new homes.

The city also connects its residents with fix-it clinics. These clinics provide people with tools and tips to repair what they have instead of buying new.

Ann Arbor also hosts electronics take-back days. Residents can drop off unwanted computers, tablets, smartphones, and other electronics. Then, these devices are repaired, reused, or responsibly recycled.

Transforming Textiles
Circ

About half of all textile waste is clothing made of a cotton and polyester blend known as polycotton. Recycling polycotton is difficult because of the way the two substances are blended.

A company called Circ is aiming to change that. It uses water, heat, pressure, and safe chemicals to separate polyester from cotton without damage. This allows both types of material to then be spun into new fabric. By 2030, Circ will be able to recycle 330,000 tn. (300,000 t) of textiles annually.

> It takes 200 years for polycotton to break down in a landfill. When burned in incinerators, the fabric releases heat-trapping carbon dioxide and other poisonous chemicals.

Circ has partnered with several popular clothing brands, including Zara.

From Table to Farm
Sanergy

We trash a lot of uneaten food, but a company named Sanergy funnels food waste back into the fields. Its Regen **Organics** program gathers food waste from restaurants, businesses, and markets. It then feeds this waste to soldier fly larvae. The bugs help convert the waste into organic **fertilizer** that can be used to grow new food. Eventually, these larvae become food themselves. They are turned into a high-protein feed for farm animals. All this work prevents 55,000 tn. (50,000 t) of organic waste from entering landfills every year, helping to offset greenhouse gas emissions.

> Sanergy's fertilizer and feed is used by more than 6,000 farmers annually. This fertilizer made from food waste boosts crop yields by up to 30 percent.

Seaweed Solutions
Notpla

Plastics—especially single-use items—are everywhere, causing harm around the world. A company called Notpla is working on a solution. It has developed a plastic alternative made from seaweed. This material can be used to make takeout containers, cutlery, and paper products. Unlike plastic, Notpla containers break down without releasing poisonous chemicals. Some Notpla products can be composted and others will dissolve in water. The company even makes a plastic alternative that can be eaten!

> The seaweed farmed by Notpla also helps reduce greenhouse gases. As it grows, the seaweed pulls heat-trapping carbon dioxide out of the atmosphere.

These Notpla takeout containers can be composted.

SEAWEED.
NOT PLASTIC.

FIND OUT HOW YOU'RE HELPING THE PLANET
↓

finally a box that is truly

MADE TO BIODEGRADE

~~plastic~~ ☐   seaweed ☑

NOTPLA

25

Waste Not, Want Not

Sometimes, it can feel like we are drowning in the stuff we buy and then throw away. But all around the world, people are making a difference. By being more conscious of what we use, we can move toward a cleaner, greener future. When we make fewer things, we save more natural resources and keep our environment cleaner. When it comes to waste, less is more . . . for everyone!

By 2032, the Danish island of Bornholm aims to become a zero-waste society. It plans to close its landfill and incinerator. Instead, all waste will be composted, recycled, reused, or repaired.

Minimize Waste!

There are lots of easy ways you can reduce how many new items you use—and how much you waste. By doing so, you will protect the planet and improve the health of all living things.

Some waste is turned to art.

Choose alternatives to single-use plastics. Carry a reusable water bottle and cloth shopping bag.

Recycle all your paper, metal, and plastic waste.

When something becomes broken or worn out, do not throw it away. Try to repurpose, recycle, or repair it.

Buy second-hand items whenever possible.

Donate unopened food that your family won't eat before it expires. Bringing it to a local food pantry helps your neighbors in need.

Glossary

atmosphere the layer of gases that surrounds Earth

carbon dioxide an invisible gas in the air that is released when fossil fuels are burned

composting turning plant and food waste into soil

decomposing rotting or breaking down

disposed gotten rid of, often by throwing away

emissions substances, such as gases and soot, released into the air by fuel-burning engines

fertilizer a substance added to soil to make plants grow better

fossil fuels sources of energy made from the remains of animals and plants that lived long ago

incinerators furnaces for burning garbage

landfills huge holes in the ground where trash is put and often buried

leaching dissolving into or leaking out from

methane a greenhouse gas that can come from rotting waste

nonrenewable not able to be replaced by a natural process in a short period of time

organics relating to or made from something once living, such as plant material

textiles woven or knit cloths

toxic poisonous and potentially deadly

Read More

Bergin, Raymond. *Decreasing Space Junk (Save Our Earth! Climate Action Explained).* Minneapolis: Bearport Publishing Company, 2026.

Donnelly, Rebecca. *Total Garbage: A Messy Dive into Trash, Waste, and Our World.* New York: Henry Holt and Company, 2023.

Feldstein, Stephanie. *How Fast Fashion Changed the World (Planet Human).* Ann Arbor, MI: Cherry Lake Publishing, 2024.

Twiddy, Robin. *Living Zero Waste (Small Steps to Save the World).* Buffalo, NY: Enslow Publishing, 2023.

Learn More Online

1. Go to **FactSurfer.com** or scan the QR code below.
2. Enter "**Minimizing Waste**" into the search box.
3. Click on the cover of this book to see a list of websites.

Index

Ann Arbor, Michigan 18
atmosphere 8, 24
carbon dioxide 8, 12, 20, 24
Circ 20
circular economy 16
climate change 8
clothes 6, 10, 18, 20, 29
composting 16, 24, 26
emissions 12, 18, 22
energy 8, 10
food 4, 8, 12, 16, 22, 29
fossil fuels 6, 8, 15
greenhouse gases 8, 12, 18, 22, 24
incinerators 4, 20, 26
landfills 4, 15, 18, 20, 22, 26

methane 12
natural resources 6, 8, 21, 26
Netherlands 16
Notpla 24–25
plastic 6, 14–16, 24, 29
recycle 10, 15–16, 18, 20, 26, 29
Regen Organics 22
repair 16, 18, 26, 29
repurpose 10, 16, 29
reuse 10, 16, 18, 26
Sanergy 22
single-use plastics 14–15, 24, 29
textiles 10, 20

About the Author

Raymond Bergin is a writer who lives in New Jersey and Massachusetts. He and his family enthusiastically compost food waste, recycle their packaging, donate unwanted clothes, shop at secondhand stores, and take advantage of reusable products.